■SCHOLASTIC
News
Nonfiction Readers

Dinosaur Armor

by Susan H. Gray

Children's Press®
A Division of Scholastic Inc.
New York Toronto London Auckland Sydney
Mexico City New Delhi Hong Kong
Danbury, Connecticut

These content vocabulary word builders are for grades 1–2.

Subject Consultant: Rudyard W. Sadleir, Doctoral Candidate in Evolutionary Biology, University of Chicago, Chicago, Illinois

Reading Consultant: Cecilia Minden-Cupp, PhD, Former Director of the Language and Literacy Program, Harvard Graduate School of Education, Cambridge, Massachusetts

Photographs © 2007: Alamy Images/Papilio: 23 bottom right; Corbis Images/Joe McDonald: 23 bottom left; JupiterImages/Highlights for Children: 2, 5 top right, 9, 19, 21 bottom, 21 top; Natural History Museum, London: 4 bottom left, 15 (Anness Publishing), 4 top, 5 top left, 14, 17 (De Agostini), 21 center (Kokoro Dreams); Photo Researchers, NY: 4 bottom right, 8 (Christian Darkin), 20 (Mark Garlick), cover, 5 bottom left, 11, 12 (Francois Gohier), 1, 7 (Christian Jegou/Publiphoto), 23 top right (John Serrao); The Image Works: 23 top left (Kike Calvo/V&W), back cover, 5 bottom right, 13 (Eastcott-Momatiuk).

Book Design: Simonsays Design!
Book Production: The Design Lab

Library of Congress Cataloging-in-Publication Data
Gray, Susan Heinrichs.
Dinosaur armor / by Susan H. Gray.
     p. cm. — (Scholastic news nonfiction readers)
Includes bibliographical references and index.
ISBN-13: 978-0-531-17481-4
ISBN-10: 0-531-17481-6
1. Ornithischia—Juvenile literature. I. Title. II. Series.
QE862.O65G74525 2007
567.9—dc22   *400 5821*   2006024051

1 2 3 4 5 6 7 8 9 10 R 16 15 14 13 12 11 10 09 08 07

CONTENTS

WORD HUNT

Look for these words as you read. They will be in **bold**.

ankylosaurids
(**ang**-kuh-luh-**sawr**-idz)

nodosaurids
(**no**-duh-**sawr**-idz)

predators
(**pred**-uh-turz)

4

carnivore
(**kar**-nih-vor)

herbivores
(**ur**-bih-vorz)

scutes
(skoots)

stegosaurids
(**steg**-uh-**sawr**-idz)

JUST THE THING

The armored dinosaurs had no fierce claws.

They had no sharp teeth.

They could not race away from danger.

They were too big to hide.

They needed *something* for protection. Armor was just the thing!

Ankylosaurus didn't have sharp teeth or claws. How do you think it protected itself?

Jégou.

Many dinosaurs were **herbivores**, or plant-eaters. They spent most of their time eating plants.

Many of these dinosaurs were also big and slow. They made great meals for **predators**, animals that hunt and eat other animals.

predator

Saltasaurus was big and slow. It probably spent most of its time eating plants.

How could these big, slow dinosaurs protect themselves from the teeth and claws of predators?

They had hard, knobby plates in their backs. They had armor! The armor helped protect them from other dinosaurs.

This skeleton clearly shows the armor of *Ankylosaurus*.

The **stegosaurids** had tall plates along their backs. Stegosaurids also had armor along their throat and hips. This armor was made up of bony **scutes**, or plates, built into their skin.

scute

The tall plates on the back of *Stegosaurus* may have helped scare away other dinosaurs.

Another group of dinosaurs, the **nodosaurids**, was covered with armor. Nodosaurids had plates on their heads, bodies, and tails.

Many of their plates had spikes. No **carnivore**, or meat-eater, could easily chomp on these dinosaurs!

carnivore

Sauropelta was a nodosaurid that lived in what is now the western United States.

Other dinosaurs, the **ankylosaurids**, were covered in armor, too. One ankylosaurid, *Euoplocephalus*, even had scutes on its eyelids!

But if all of that armor didn't keep predators away, ankylosaurids also had a great weapon. They had a club at the end of their tail!

Euoplocephalus had scutes, spikes, horns, and a club at the end of its tail.

Some dinosaurs had hard plates covering their bodies.

Others had big spikes.

Many had both!

There were many different kinds of armor.

But they were all good at protecting dinosaurs against predators.

Edmontonia had lots of armor and long spikes on its sides.

ARMOR OR WEAPON? YOU DECIDE!

There are no dinosaurs alive today, so we can only guess at how they lived. Take a look at these body parts and decide if you think they were used as armor for protection or as weapons.

Tail spikes on a stegosaurid

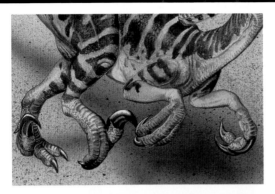

Foot and hand claws of a predator

Body or head plates of *Ankylosaurus*

Horns of *Triceratops*

YOUR NEW WORDS

ankylosaurids (**ang**-kuh-luh-**sawr**-idz) dinosaurs covered with plates and having a tail club

carnivore (**kar**-nih-vor) an animal that eats meat

herbivores (**ur**-bih-vorz) animals that eat plants

nodosaurids (**no**-duh-**sawr**-idz) dinosaurs covered with plates but no tail club

predators (**pred**-uh-turz) animals that hunt other animals for food

scutes (skoots) plates or disks

stegosaurids (**steg**-uh-**sawr**-idz) armored dinosaurs with tall plates running down their backs and with spikes on their tails

OTHER ANIMALS WITH ARMOR

armadillo

crab

pill bug

turtle

23

INDEX

FIND OUT MORE

Book:

Mattern, Joanne. *Dinosaur Tails and Armor.* Milwaukee: Weekly Reader Early Learning Library, 2005.

Website:

ZoomDinosaurs.com
http://www.enchantedlearning.com/subjects/dinosaurs

MEET THE AUTHOR

Susan H. Gray has a master's degree in zoology. She has written more than seventy science and reference books for children. She especially loves to write about animals. Susan and her husband, Michael, live in Cabot, Arkansas.

EMMA S. CLARK MEMORIAL LIBRARY

SETAUKET, NEW YORK 11733